Resisting Temptation

Colin N. Peckham

CHRISTIAN FOCUS

All scripture quotations, unless otherwise indicated, are taken from the New King James Version. Copyright © 1982 by Thomas Nelson, Inc. Used by permission. All rights reserved.

© Colin N. Peckham

ISBN 1-85792-247-6

10 9 8 7 6 5 4 3 2 1

First published in 1999
Reprinted 2005
by
Christian Focus Publications,
Geanies House, Fearn, Tain, Ross-shire,
IV20 1TW, Scotland

www.christianfocus.com

Cover design by
Alister MacInnes

Printed and bound by
Nørhaven Paperback A/S, Denmark

All rights reserved. No part of this publication may be reproduced, stored in a retrieval system, or transmitted, in any form, by any means, electronic, mechanical, photocopying, recording or otherwise without the prior permission of the publisher or a license permitting restricted copying. In the U.K. such licenses are issued by the Copyright Licensing Agency, 90 Tottenham Court Road, London W1P 9HE.

Resisting Temptation

Rev. Dr. Colin N. Peckham, LTh Hons, BA, (Theol), BTh Hons, MTh, DTh, was born in South Africa where he had ten years of evangelistic ministry and youth work before entering Bible College work in Cape Town. For seventeen years he was Principal of The Faith Mission Bible College, Edinburgh, Scotland. He is now Principal Emeritas of this college and has a wide-ranging preaching ministry in Britain, America, Africa and other areas of the world.

Contents

Setting the Scene

Because of the increasing prevalence of infidelity and immorality in Christian circles, I have decided to write a few words on this important subject. They are words of warning, not from a lofty tower of inaccessibility but from a man among men.

Robert Burns said long ago, 'A man's a man for a' that.' All are vulnerable; all can fall; all can face ruin because of improper sexual relationships. Compromise in morality can sabotage our ministry. No-one is immune from attraction to someone else. Sadly, across the lives of some who were in the Christian ministry has been written that tragic word 'fallen'. I point no finger. I thank God for His gracious hand of protection on my life keeping me clean, but I bow humbly and pray, for I also am a man, and 'a man's a man for a' that'. May God protect us all.

First of all, it is necessary to establish biblical principles. The Bible gives absolute standards: 'You shall not commit adultery' (Ex. 20:14). According to Levitical law, 'The adulterer and the adulteress shall surely be put to death' (Lev. 20:10). The New Testament is also clear: 'Do not be deceived. Neither fornicators...nor adulterers...shall inherit the kingdom of God' (1 Cor. 6: 9,10).

By definition, adultery is voluntary sexual intercourse between a married man or a married woman and someone outside of the marriage bond – an extra-marital sexual relationship.

Fornication is voluntary sexual intercourse between unmarried people – a premarital sexual relationship. This immorality has left the dark caverns of censured wickedness and has become largely the accepted norm in modern society. The Church in its turn has become conditioned to the lowered standards.

We have become so used to hearing of people in immoral situations that it no longer offends us. The standards of the world invade the church merely eliciting disapproving shrugs or sighs accompanied by the remark, 'Well, that's how it is these days!' But God has not changed, and His demands for moral purity have not changed. The world may have eroded biblical standards but the inexorable command is still there, 'Thou shalt not commit adultery!' To Him we must give account.

Nothing so destroys the foundation of marriage as immorality. Its disastrous power demolishes a person's worth. It nullifies trust, destroys respect and integrity, brings shame and grief, and devastates self-esteem. It defrauds people, reducing them to objects of use, not love. An immoral relationship is not an expression of love, but a revelation of selfish lust. Lust is a beast that can devour us. Love desires the best for another person, and endures pain, sacrificing selfish gratification for the good of the other. We live however, in a selfish world that demands that self must be gratified whatever the cost to others. Immorality takes place; the families suffer, the children suffer, the Christian witness suffers, Christ suffers!

Immorality does not occur overnight. We are not paragons of virtue one day and engaging in immorality the next. We are gradually conditioned to it by the media until it becomes inoffensive. Then inappropriate dress, unwise demeanour, provocative talk and subtle teasing lower further our defences.

Slowly protective values are eroded and improper bridges are built. The lingering look, the telling touch, the long handshake, the overlong arm squeeze, the hand on the shoulder, the close-contact conversation, the understanding and sympathetic friendship, each act contributing to building an improper relationship.

The heart quickens, fantasies chase one another through the mind, the imagination runs riot. Mental images and reveries accumulate and dominate. Slowly the net is spread; gradually, imperceptibly, the line is crossed. Conversations of a personal nature increase. Dependence upon one another increases. The warning lights flicker but grow fainter and dimmer. Excuses are made to be together; lies are told. The inner warning voice has been effectively stilled. You rationalize your behaviour: 'He/she needs me'; 'We minister together'. You argue away the improper attitudes and conduct, pretending they don't exist: 'There is no damage'; 'We are Christians'; 'The Lord is protecting us and blessing us'; 'It's so helpful to the work of God for us to work together in this way.'

A good and friendly relationship has advanced to inappropriate emotional dependence. You are emotionally involved. You live in a painful world between fantasy and reality. It is a kind of spiritual adultery. It is moving relentlessly forward.

One day, one fateful day, the desires and the opportunities coincide and what was conceived by contact and conversation, by fantasy and foolishness, now actually takes place. Thoughts have inevitably led to actions and now the consequences must be faced.

Another devastating tragedy takes place. The church must live through it somehow. Another crippling humiliation, another series of broken lives and grief-stricken hearts. What a sad and sickening calamity.

May God help us in some small measure to stem the tide of Satanically-inspired infidelity.

Temptation

Temptation is the common lot of men; we are targets for Satan. Adam and Eve in their original holiness were tempted. Jesus Christ, God's Son, as representative of man was supremely tempted. Temptation probed the depths of His being, and He 'suffered, being tempted' (Heb. 2:18). We too experience trouble and heaviness in temptation. Peter acknowledges this by saying, 'ye have been grieved by various trials' (1 Pet. 1:6). We must not be engulfed by confusion and think that the very sinking of spirits in temptation is itself sin. This only weakens our defence and makes us more vulnerable to sin.

Temptation is a testing designed to strengthen or corrupt. Satan uses a variety of temptations according to our personality and background. Man's five senses come into contact with an evil world and these become avenues of temptation.

Temptation can develop our strength: 'The testing of your faith produces patience' (Jas. 1:3). The Greek speaks of the testing of your faith working out or developing endurance or perseverance. The Revised Standard Version says that it 'produces steadfastness'. A raw army recruit must be trained and tested before he can play an active part in the battle. A Christian who has not learned to overcome temptation is of little value to the cause of Christ. Faith develops perseverance in the test so that we may be 'mature and complete, not lacking anything' (James 1:4, Greek). God makes us strong in and through the temptation. Think of it! Even in the midst of the vilest temptation we can be strengthened and emerge victorious. Temptation certainly comes from the devil, but it is permitted by God for our good. As we meet and overcome temptation we can grow in stature and strength.

Temptation affects the human race in three basic forms: the world, the flesh and the devil – the trinity of evil. This is seen in 1 John 2:15 where we are commanded not to love the world, neither the things that are in the world. These are represented under three headings: 'The lust of the flesh, the lust of the eyes, and the pride of life' (1 John 2:16). They are afterwards reduced to one, the lust of the world (verse 17).

This could be related to the temptation in the Garden of Eden (Gen. 3:14-19), the forbidden fruit representing the world, the appetite that lusted after the fruit representing the flesh, the agent used to attract attention to the fruit, representing the devil. Eve rightly opposed the tempter with 'God has said' (Gen. 3:3), but unfortunately did not persist in her course. Later Jesus said it and held firm. In Romans 13:14 we are commanded to make no provision for the flesh, but Eve sought to make provision for herself, and thus fell in the temptation of the devil.

Another picture of the trinity of evil is given in Matthew 4 where Jesus is tempted to work a miracle to gratify the flesh, to take a short-cut to gain His rightful position as ruler of the world, to bow down and worship the devil. Jesus is our example in that in trying circumstances He trusted in God and waited, being guided and sustained by what was written. He met every temptation by a quotation from Scripture. The Father's word was to Him the sword with which He routed the great spiritual enemy who is ever plotting our ruin. Here we see the value of the Scripture and the impotence of Satan against it. The devil may tempt us to fall, but he cannot make us fall. He may persuade us to cast ourselves down but he cannot cast us down.

Yet another picture of this evil alliance is seen in Ephesians 2:2-3 where we read of the course of this world, the lusts and desires of the flesh, and the prince of the power of the air.

Lust signifies selfish desire and John gives us three realms in which it operates appealing to man's selfish desires.

1. The Lust of the Flesh

Here we judge everything by material standards and live a life which is dominated by the senses. Whilst it is right to satisfy a legitimate appetite, such as that of sex within the confines of the marriage bond, it is wrong to let that appetite have free reign. To live a sensuous life is to be, amongst other things, lustful and lax in morals. Fleshly desires creep into our affections as an angel of light. We are selfishly unwilling to give them up, and enjoy a pleasant feeling of satisfaction and a growing impatience of any interruption of that enjoyment. Soon legitimate appreciation for an unavailable person turns into selfishness and sin. Natural desires become unholy lust as our natural appetites are perverted and debased. The discipline and control of the body and its appetites slip away and we slide into a dangerous realm of yielding to the lusts of the flesh.

2. The Lust of the Eyes

We have here a place of vulnerable temptation. As one walks in the streets or on the beaches one is conscious of the violent assaults made upon the eye-gate. Modern advertising uses the female form to sell everything. What the eye sees and gloats over, the heart will soon passionately desire. There is first of all *discovery* as the eye holds the magic. This is translated very soon into *desire*. As the soul further yields to temptation, the body, the temple of the Lord, is *desecrated* by the impurity which was imported originally through the eye-gate. Thoughts are defiled. Television, magazines and the press, are calculated to *degrade* the minds and smear the heart. Sex appeal is lauded as love, vice is made attractive; dress (or the lack of it) may be indecent and immoral. These things we see, and our imagination can run riot.

Eve saw the tree as a delight to the eyes. It fascinated her, stirred her, gripped her imagination and urged a desire for the fruit. She yielded with the direst of consequences. Achan said: '*I saw ... I coveted ... took ... hid*' (Josh. 7:21), and he received just punishment for his disobedience and sin. The process begins with the eye gate. David's lustful looking at Bathsheba as she bathed is another example (2 Sam. 11:2). What sin followed! What sorrow it brought to his repentant heart, and what tragic results it had in his family. Yielding to lust leads the soul to disaster and tragedy.

3. The Pride of Life

This term speaks of the vainglory of life, or life's empty pride. It means to claim for yourself possessions, deeds and achievements which do not belong to you, in order to impress others and to exalt yourself.

Satan therefore attracts us with corrupt values, covetous desires and arrogant vanity. We must learn to expect the constant pressures of temptation and be alert to new forms and approaches throughout life. Every inch of ground will be contested by the enemy.

Fortunately God knows 'how to deliver the godly out of temptations' (2 Pet. 2:9). He warns us to 'watch and pray' so that we don't 'enter ... into temptation' (Matt. 26:41). He urges us to 'stand fast ... in the liberty by which Christ has made us free' (Gal. 5:1). Jesus has Himself suffered in temptation, and is 'able to aid those who are tempted' (Heb. 2:18). He gives a marvellous word to us in 1 Corinthians 10:13. Let it speak to the tempest-tossed, struggling Christian today. Note the wording in J. B. Phillip's paraphrase: 'No temptation has come your way that is too hard for flesh and blood to bear. But God can be trusted not to allow you to suffer any temptation beyond your powers of endurance. He will see to it that every temptation has a way out, so that it will never be impossible for you to bear it.' God can be trusted!

There is an old hymn that has comforted and strengthened the Church for nearly two centuries. It promises:

> The soul that on Jesus hath leaned for repose,
> I will not, I will not desert to his foes,
> That soul, tho' all hell should endeavour to
>   shake,
> I'll never, no never, no never forsake!

Danger Areas

Working
The place of employment is an area of great vulnerability.

A respected Bible College principal in London advised his students to 'work on the assumption that the devil has planted a member of the opposite sex where you work to trap you'.

In the workplace, people have similar interests and concerns. There is the same pressure to perform, to excel. There is close co-operation in projects which sometimes fail, resulting in commiseration together; and which sometimes succeed, resulting in celebration together. There is fellow-feeling, camaraderie, unity, purpose, excitement, electricity, vibes! Men and women are performing at their best, dressed and polished to the teeth. They are thrown together for more hours of interactive and purposeful living than those spent with their spouse. They see each other very differently to the way in which the wife at home sees her weary husband. She is aware of all the faults that intimacy reveals and would not suspect that anyone would fall for her man. She in turn is not dressed and groomed to kill and has perhaps lost her sparkle in the weariness of raising three children. She is still in bed when he leaves the house and is embroiled in household duties till he returns. Comparisons are made. Those bright and enthusiastic girls at the office are now seen in a desirable light. They understand the hurt of a failed business deal far better than the wife and can console more meaningfully. There is a natural fulfilment in their presence, far more so than the wife with whom he spends much less effective time. The scene is set for moral disaster.

The danger is not merely confined to the married man, but extends as well to the working woman. Some men at work are on the prowl and some are on the lookout for sexual adventures.

How do we combat this inexorable pressure?

Recognize the potential danger of the workplace. Conversations in the workplace should not include personal problems. Don't discuss the failure of your spouse at the office. This will evoke a sympathetic response from those who feel that they could make you happy when your spouse is obviously not doing so. Don't lean on the unavailable person. This is a language which the sexually adventurous will understand. Don't tease with subtle insinuations, nor ask provocative questions. Don't stare with meaningful, lingering looks.

The wife at home must realize that her husband is stepping into a minefield, for ours is a sex-mad society. She should take a serious interest in her personal appearance. She should also take a keen interest in his work, and as far as it is possible, feel with him in it. Remember, if he is not appreciated at home, he is at work.

Guard the relationship between husband and wife. If difficulties arise here, major problems may ensue. If one party feels always 'put down', taken for granted, despised, unloved; should harsh words and unkind comments, discourtesy, insensitivity, inconsideration be the order of the day, the way is wide open for the aggrieved party to respond to anyone showing sympathy, appreciation and kindness. Should sexual contact between them be severed, either party could turn elsewhere. Overlong separations between husband and wife could have the same effect.

Meaningful time spent together, and with the children, is absolutely essential. This gives a base and foundation and makes anyone think twice before launching into something that would deprive them of the beauty and harmony of a fulfilling, comforting and happy home.

Visiting

For the pastor or Christian worker this is an exceedingly dangerous area. People love to have the minister in their homes. It enables them to chat together in an informal atmosphere and to reciprocate kindness to the one from whom they receive so much instruction and help.

The following remarks should not take the happy spontaneity out of a pleasant visit, nor should they be regarded as legalistic in any way. As friendly relationships develop, friendly gestures are exchanged and sometimes motherly or fatherly instincts are evident in kind and reciprocated pleasantries. Many happy remarks, gestures and touches are totally innocent and guileless and are simply part of the ongoing texture of life. Sometimes a hug in the presence of others is altogether appropriate and innocent and can be an encouragement to the recipient.

Care should be taken however, in the visitation programme of the Christian worker, for sometimes it is necessary to visit when the husband is not there. If possible take someone else with you. If not possible, be circumspect and discreet, not staying any longer than necessary. When invited to sit down try to avoid sitting on a settee which holds more than one person. Choose a chair, if possible, which is separate from the others. As soon as possible, open the Bible for instruction, so that should any-one come into the room, your intentions would be obvious. Should a coffee table be between you and the lady of the house, it would be all to the good. If you are alone it would be unwise to put your arm sympathetically around her shoulders, or hold her arm, or make any other sympathetic physical con-tact. Limit your conversation to the matter in hand and not to numerous time-consuming anecdotes and unrelated incidents. Keep the door of the room ajar.

Counselling
This is the area where Christian workers are most vulnerable.

Many of the principles mentioned above apply here as well. If possible ladies should counsel ladies and men should counsel men. This is to be strongly advised. At times this rule will have to be broken and men will have to counsel ladies and vice versa.

If the counselling is done in a church or hall it is helpful to place your Bible on the pew between the counsellee and yourself. This prevents unnecessary proximity. It may seem foolish and unnecessary, but when one looks at the moral catastrophes all around, little precautions like this are sensible defences to avoid similar possible failures.

Don't counsel someone from the opposite sex for long periods at a time. Ascertain the problem and arrange for them to see someone appropriate of their own sex. Don't counsel someone of the opposite sex at length after the night meeting. If you have to do so, ask someone else to sit at the back of the church whilst you chat at the front. Don't sit in the car together and talk about the problem, particularly at night. Take care lest any word or action be misinterpreted causing the counsellee to suspect improper motives. Further counselling could lead to disaster if this were the case.

Travelling

This is another area of special vulnerability. You are unknown and not accountable to anyone locally. Lonely flights, lonely journeys, lonely dinners, lonely rooms – and the scene is set for temptation. Some hotels have seductive surroundings often with romantic music and intriguing settings. Travel affords a particular area of temptation. To be forewarned is to be forearmed.

An evangelist friend told how a little while after being shown to his hotel room, a member of the

hotel staff knocked at his door, charmingly introduced herself and told him that God had sent her to
him for the night. He said that he did the only thing
he could; he grabbed his case and fled, spending
the night at another hotel.

Pastor/Secretary relationship

Of particular importance in Christian service is the
place of the secretary in the local church or in the
mission office. In some instances, the secretary
stays on the mission compound or in the home of
the missionary family and becomes an all-purpose
helper in the advance of their Christian cause. They
pray together, dream together, plan together. They
see the work growing and are thrilled with the bless-
ings and possibilities.

They give themselves to the service of God and
in this service, the relationship, which was one of
good friendliness and mutual respect, may grow
into something inappropriate. There is nothing
physical, so it is not regarded as dangerous or even
suspicious. It is justified as unity of purpose and
objective – all for the glory of God.

He is the only man she sees constantly and to
whom she looks for guidance and instruction. She
relates her work to his requirements and desires.
Her life is being wound around his. She responds to
his likes and dislikes and thinks about him a great

deal of the time. A work dependency has grown into an emotional dependency.

She is only a part of his life, for he has a wife and family, but he is the centre of hers. He could never be more than a friend but her life is now so entwined in his that she is emotionally involved and bound up in an unhealthy and unfulfilling emotional dependency. This whole affair can be very painful, and sometimes the only way to handle it is for the secretary to find other lodgings if she had been staying with the couple, or to leave the work completely and join another branch of Christian service.

To prevent this build-up to unacceptable levels of dependency, the secretary should fill her life with interests other than those of the church or mission society. Let her join a choir, teach a Sunday School class, learn to play an instrument, interact with a circle of friends outside the confined group. She must broaden her interests and live her own life. This safeguards her, the family and the work of the Lord, for, once caught up in the trap of emotional dependence it may well take a long time to break free, and scars from such a frustrating, futile and hurtful relationship may be carried for years.

There are many happy and profitable relationships in church offices but it is possible for the church secretary to be placed in a vulnerable position on some occasions. Should a potentially dangerous phase emerge, weekly programmes could be altered, or voluntary helpers could breeze in and neutralize the risk.

A pastor's wife became ill, and later, because of misunderstandings and estrangements she and her husband grew apart. Although occupying the same house, they had virtually no physical contact. For years he had an excellent and irreproachable relationship with his highly efficient secretary who not only organized much of the church work, but also typed the books he wrote. The loneliness and sadness of his frustrated private life bore in upon him, and one fateful day, when particularly low in spirits, the tragedy occurred. After seventeen unblemished years of exemplary co-operation, suddenly, in half-an-hour his life was in ruins. He was utterly devastated by sorrow, remorse and re-pentance. Eventually he divorced his wife, married his secretary and retired from active Christian serv-ice. His gifts were such, however, that churches in time, albeit apprehensively at first, invited him to minister. He limped back into Christian service and after some years gained a measure of con-fidence again, sorrowing till he died for what he described as 'the cloud that overshadows my life'. Had his relationship with his wife been happy and fulfilling, this tragedy would probably never have occurred.

Church Relationships

Many extramarital affairs are not sexually motivated, even though that becomes the ultimate result. As human beings we have a desire for fellowship and intimacy, and it is just here that the path to adultery in Christian marriages can slip in under the radar.

Not only are our deepest longings for intimacy filled by God, but on another level we long for the love, respect and intimacy of another human being. Spiritual and emotional rapport is what Christian fellowship is all about, and this is a critical element in the Christian adultery trap.

Church home groups are numerous and they help to make the church a vibrant, active, thriving body, but harmful dangers lurk in the intimacy and camaraderie of that close-knit fellowship. Someone of the opposite sex can helpfully work through a crisis with you and a bonding takes place which is wonderful if kept on the level of fellowship and is not allowed to develop further. Christian fellowship and an 'affair' obviously differ in depth and substance, but the intimate nature of emotional rapport is not easy to control.

James had problems at work and his frustrations were not grasped nor understood by his wife. He shared his problems at the home fellowship group and they prayed for him. Afterwards over the tea-cups Susan told him that she had had similar problems and could really identify with his situation. A few weeks later Susan came in late and the only seat was next to James. They chatted about the problem once again, and then Susan asked his advice about something with which she was battling. He seemed to have such insight into it all, that at various functions it became quite natural to seek one another out. Soon they were sharing along deeper lines and their families were mentioned with problems emerging. At a church picnic, in all the fun, suddenly James saw her in a different light. They had helped one another in true Christian fellowship, but now suddenly a spark of sexuality was introduced. He sensed that the feelings were mutual. That which was appropriate, above board, and helpful, now became exceedingly dangerous and potentially destructive. Alarm bells should be ringing and red lights flashing at this stage. They were entering the danger zone where the will could show signs of fatigue, where they would desire not only advice and help, but each other. (How many times could this situation be repeated!).

At this stage it is necessary to step back from each other, to determinedly steer clear of each other's company, to be involved in a crowd when the other person is present, to stop asking advice from one another, to stop phoning each other. Break the contact. God teaches us to deny ungodliness and worldly lusts (Titus 2:11-12). Self-control is the fruit of the Spirit, but *we* must implement God's command. Our responsibility is to obey God, and we will find that His Spirit comes to our aid and gives us His power to do so.

Danger Times

There are times when we are more vulnerable than at other times. When our stable world is threatened, when the equilibrium of our lives is upset, when we are weary and worn, burdened and battered by the storms of life, when we suffer 'the slings and arrows of outrageous fortune', when we are crushed by failure, endure the strains and stresses of teenage tantrums and traumas at home, or experience new circumstances at work – we are vulnerable. A combination of these factors with perhaps a period of loneliness or disharmony at home could ease us into the comfort which an interested bystander could give, resulting in a gratifying but disastrous relationship.

Discouragement is one of the greatest pathways to temptation. Of course it is right and necessary to encourage but care must be taken and a strict vigilance observed so that the helping hand is not permanently taken.

Two church workers might be labouring together, one with more counselling ability than the other. People throng to A for help while B feels neglected and worthless. B could easily weep on a sympathetic shoulder with sad consequences.

Two preachers may be in nearby churches. The one with the greater gifts draws people away from the other whose self-image receives a sickening blow. This could be lessened and healed by the comfort of a devoted deaconess or church worker who senses his need and encourages him warmly. Both preacher and deaconess are vulnerable and friendship's bond could easily lead into forbidden territory.

A young dynamic pastor might be appointed who totally eclipses the older, faithful man, who now needs his wife to encourage him and assure him that he is still a useful member of Christ's church. Comfort given at this vulnerable point in his life by someone else could upset the balance and end in disaster.

A married man may not be making a success of his job. He is not being appreciated and feels hurt and defeated. If someone in the office were to show him that he really has got what it takes, that he can rise to meet the challenge and lift his head again, the caring compliments could restore self-esteem and forge a new bond which could lead to interdependence and strong temptation.

The end of a relationship is another moment of vulnerability. Someone is needed to help you through the trauma. Choose your friend well. Be careful that you don't become embroiled with a married person and end up worse than at the beginning. A lady had a loving relationship with her husband. Together they helped a mutual friend through the trauma of her divorce. The lady had to leave her husband and two teenage children for a family reunion for two weeks. When she returned, she found that he had moved out and was living with the other woman. The shock caused their son to fail his final examinations, and as a result, abandon the expected university career. Another shattered family.

Don't deceive yourself into thinking that you are strong and do not need warm companionship. You may feel that your church work and spiritual activities are so fulfilling that you can make it on your own. *Loneliness*, however, is a force to be reckoned with. You need others, but take care that this need is not filled by someone who may so easily slip in and lead you further than you want to go. The road back is very painful.

So many are under *stress* today – stress of all kinds. To some, house-moving is a traumatic experience. There are tensions when finances are low, when teenagers assert their rights – selfishly, lazily and untidily. And oh, the music and its decibels, the friends and their habits! Then there is the weariness brought on by overwork and the pressures of life – the utter weariness of body and spirit. Stress and weariness must be alleviated somehow – perhaps by an evening out with someone who understands. The sympathy and friendship shown at such a time must be closely guarded. Remember, in weakness and tensions you are vulnerable!

Suddenly at forty-eight the dreams you had are seen to be unrealizable. They will not be fulfilled. Youth has fled away. A *mid-life crisis* develops. The woman sees the lines on her face, the rounding form. The man sees his balding head and knows that the bright prospects of life have slipped away and are but stark impossibilities. There is a need – a need which can be met by someone who would take time and patience to sit and talk – and then?!

Success is another state which leads to immorality. Flushed with victory, acceptance, the heady moments of glory, it is easy to embrace, to laugh together with others, to talk enthusiastically. Pride rears it head: 'It could never happen to me – just look how the Lord has blessed me.' Just at that crucial point of victory it can happen! Pride comes before a fall.

Sometimes interest in others becomes a two-edged sword. When the man shows an interest in another women, his wife may be driven by *jealousy* and sheer devilment to show him that two can play at that game. She casts her eyes in the direction of another, and soon they are all caught up in the ghastly whirlpool of turmoil and tragedy.

How to Escape – Practically

When there is a particular *chemistry* between you and an unavailable person, *recognize it*. Take note of the kind of person with whom you like to keep company and be forewarned that the enjoyable chatter and fun is not allowed to extend beyond the acceptable. We just 'click' with some people and it is natural to extend special friendship to them and to spend more time with them, as we recognize their qualities and appreciate their worth.

Remember too, that there are not only physical attractions, but those of character, of wisdom, of compassion, of spirituality. You can easily be caught up in a desire to be better instructed, or to receive or give spiritual help to the person. You can help them through their problems, real or imaginary and they appreciate your help. But when interest quickens there are always more problems to solve and more advice to give. There are dangers long before the physical is ever reached. Change your behaviour patterns if you sense the danger signals. If it is getting too strong, the only solution may be a geographical change to prevent tragedy. Withdraw and leave the other party in the hands of the Lord. Keep a watch on the vulnerable area of life's relationships.

When there is *affinity* of personality and interest, there is need for *vigilance*. Christians are particularly vulnerable because their interest is the Bible and the Lord. They help one another to grow in grace, they pray together, they work together. They are delegated to various projects, such as knocking on doors, singing, testifying or speaking at meetings together. A married man may pick up an unmarried girl *en route* to the church or to a delegated meeting, and may take her home again. Repeated journeys of this nature and the joy of seeing blessing on their work together may result in unnoticed familiarity which may well lead to tragedy. It is far better to take a bus, or get a lift with someone else to prevent dangerous developments. If you have to be one of the last at the church, see that you are not there alone with someone who is unavailable. Avoid the first developments of a possible link.

The danger is that there are so many levels of communication that any of us could unknowingly be in the beginning stages of an improper relationship. There is always the possibility that it could happen to you; it could happen to me. The earlier the danger signals can be detected, the better.

Don't be exclusive in your attentions. Show the same friendliness and appreciation to all. Whilst comments on a brooch or smart attractive clothing may be fitting, yet to extend those comments to the person's beauty or personal qualities is a dangerous advance. It may well set the bells ringing and trigger all sorts of fantasies. She in turn could be flattered that you could be so intelligent and discerning as to appreciate her excellent qualities and could engineer circumstances to be with you again. A turn of events is set in motion which could end in disaster. Should you sense that it is going too far, step back straight away out of harm's way.

Face the issue when you are slipping into a relationship outside marriage, and don't try to convince yourself that the other person does not feel as you do. You could deny the possibility that the unavailable person is in love with you and continue the friendship. Your denial is but a cover for romantic advance. Don't hide behind the thinking that the other person could not possibly have similar feelings; rather assume that if you feel that way, the other person does too! If the truth be told sexual involvement is exciting. We may fool ourselves into thinking that it is innocent at first, but the feelings generated by the attraction of the opposite sex are powerful and often addictive. Be aware also that even if you may feel nothing improper, the other person may be having difficulty. Acknowledging an improper attraction is a vital first step in coming to terms with it.

Be careful about *touching*. Sometimes a touch means nothing at all. Sometimes, at a time of grief and bereavement for instance, it may be right and necessary, but sometimes, especially if it is just too long, it can be fire. It can spark off wild imaginations and emotions. Far better to avoid any physical contact, especially if there is 'chemistry'. Holding or embracing could be deemed provocative, and this is unfair, dishonest and ungodly.

Should you feel an attraction to an unavailable person, whatever you do, *don't tell them*! If you do, the relationship is placed immediately under a terrible strain. Healthy good relations are jeopardized. What is the informed person to do? Tell their spouse? What becomes of the relationship with that couple? Will they keep it quiet? Will the church soon know? Will the people soon begin to avoid you as a potential threat to marriages?

If you are caught in some sexual snare, don't speak to people about the situation, but it may be helpful to *tell some mature responsible Christian*, who will hold you accountable. You must be sure that this person can be trusted not to speak to others. Perhaps it might be wise to confide in someone away from your particular church or fellowship to ensure confidentiality. There may however, be someone of spiritual maturity in your own church who would be completely trustworthy and who would be able to help you through as you deal with the matter openly and honestly. Having to 'report back' is a salutary exercise and a stimulus to progress and healing. For men this person should not be a woman, for not only should this level of intimacy not be shared with a woman other than your wife, but also a woman cannot always see things from a male perspective. For the same reasons, a woman should confide in a woman.

Some people, particularly those who have been married and are no longer so, have experienced married love and miss it intensely. Singles will have love-hunger in varying degrees of intensity. Some are famished for love and will respond emotionally to just a look or a word, given perhaps unintentionally but taken seriously. An apparent indication of interest could lead to passionate and improper thoughts and great vulnerability. A marriage and a whole future can unfortunately be imaginatively built on a remark thoughtlessly given, which, if not followed through may result in intense censure and bitterness. Of course you can say different things to different people. *Remarks* made to one person would have no effect whatever, but to another, would set off a blazing trail of damaging imaginations and futile hopes.

Every woman knows how to *withdraw with subtlety* from threatening situations. There is the turn of the head, the clever break from engrossing conversations, the backward step, the body language, which without words and without hurt terminates the advancing communication of hearts. This needs to be put to good use.

Pornography. It is amazing that Christians would ever be involved in pornography – but some are! To buy that first pornographic magazine was a fearsome thing, but now it's much easier and does not produce the guilt it once did. Some actually find it easy to watch lurid videos or late-night TV sex shows. At first it was a terrible anxiety provoking experience, laden with guilt and shame. Should anyone come near the room the TV channel was quickly switched to prevent detection. But after a while this reaction fades. The pornography and videos provide a self-centred substitute for sex.

Some sort of bizarre gratification is enjoyed without the intimacy and commitment to another person. It is a totally selfish comfort zone which weakens our whole moral fibre and hastens our drift from spirituality. Flee pornography! Don't touch it, whether it be in magazine form or video and TV. It can only damage your walk with God, weaken your testimony and ministry, and make you vulnerable to temptation.

Sometimes when there is 'chemistry' between two folk, one of whom is married, it helps to *show interest in the spouse*, and involve him or her in thoughts and plans. This normalises behaviour, relieves suspicion, restores confidence and establishes friendships.

The man needs to *appreciate his wife*. He needs to gratefully voice his appreciation to her for all her tiresome labour behind the scenes. He needs to express pleasure at her tasty food, choice of clothes, daily choices. This is her world and she needs to know that he appreciates her there. She appreciates a touch, a look, a compliment. This is entirely scriptural, for of the virtuous woman we read, 'her husband ... praises her' (Prov. 31:28). He does not give appreciation in silence; he gives vocal expression to his appreciation! If you don't tell her how well she looks, someone else will. She would much rather have the man she loves breathe his appreciation to her. To him she can respond with warmth and joy, strengthening the bond between them.

Men and women need to *affirm their love* to one another vocally. They frequently need to say it to one another. The precious words, 'I love you,' should be spoken throughout life, and that love needs to be fostered and fanned. They need to enjoy each other and must never lose the freshness and wonder of their relationship. It is sensed in so many little ways: the glance across a crowded room, the little squeeze of the hand or arm, the happy welcome home, the meaningful courtesies and helpful little actions, the forethought and kindness, the unexpected little gift. Make time for one another, however busy the programme. Keep the home fires burning – it pays off. Nurture love and fan it into a flame.

Work at your marriage. This takes time, but investing time in your marriage pays off. The harder you work at a relationship the better it is. It's a two-way street. If you both go more than half-way, you walk further together. No loving relationship can move forward without the wheels of intimacy being lubricated frequently. This requires deliberate, intentional effort. Don't delude yourself into thinking that your marriage is so strong that it doesn't need frequent maintenance. Work at not being selfish, at being helpful to each other. Put your spouse's feelings and desires ahead of your own. Be thoughtful; be considerate; be kind; be co-operative; be responsive; be sensitive. Admit mistakes. You will never get past having to say, 'I am sorry.' Be big enough to admit that you were wrong, and say it when necessary. Forgive and forget. Don't say things in jest which cause hurt and embarrassment.

Don't constantly harp on about previous failures. We naturally tend to be most critical of those closest to us. We expect our spouse to read our needs and wants without our even verbalizing them. Then when they don't meet them we become annoyed and critical of their love and caring for us. We often have 'super human' expectations they can't possibly fulfil while looking after all the other demands in their life. In the mundaneness of marriage, one day the husband or wife may wake up to realize that they will never have what they had hoped for. They can either change their expectations or change their partner. Choosing the latter where husbands and wives are forever trying to force their partners into the mould of their own making only leads to friction and often comes out as criticism. Relationships can then be ruptured, and if, at such a time, someone else encourages and praises the one under pressure, that one could easily walk into a trap. Patience, respect and humour help smooth the rough edges.

Speak well of each other. Be courteous. Don't get into the habit of speaking rudely to one another. Don't hold back affection. Don't allow work to so dominate your lives that you have no time for each other. Share frequently about things that are important. Pursue God together. Learn to enjoy each other's company. Do things together instead of each going separate ways. Make a conscious effort to be appreciative, intimate and pleasing to your spouse. Be willing to change, adapt and give. Always maintain contact. Whatever happens, be prepared to listen to your partner without breaking in and making further conversation impossible. Communicate through the barriers. Solve the little irritations that remain unaddressed and that don't go away. If you don't, they just build in the subconscious and make one vulnerable to temptation.

Marriage is God's chosen arena in which to teach us more of Himself, therefore allow all the problems and difficulties to drive you to Him. He can produce the love needed to make the marriage a success. Build on the foundations, work at commitment as you fulfil goals and visions.

Be honest with one another. A loyal and loving wife can stand behind her husband in the ministry and rejoice in his successes and abilities. But without his suspecting it, she could be consumed by jealousy when she hears the ladies say that he is so understanding and sensitive, so approachable and helpful. She could bottle up her feelings and whisper encouragingly to him that there is not a jealous bone in her body, but all the time feel totally unfulfilled and inadequate in a partnership where he is the dominant figure, and where she is not always the recipient of his understanding. She might feel unappreciated and unacknowledged even though they spend time together. Why do those women who have problems always seem to gain his attention? Frustration with her lot may build up and eventually burst out in a serious rupture of relationships ending in the divorce courts. If only she had spoken openly and honestly all along the way he could have been more circumspect and this could have been prevented.

Consider the consequences. What a price you will have to pay if you desert your spouse for another. Think of your career in Christian work – it will lie in ruins. Trying to get a secular job with a theological degree is not that easy! Think of the work you love, the people you will disappoint, the friends who will be deeply

49

shocked, your associates in Christian work who will be desper-ately hurt, the work of God and the name of Christ which will be dishonoured. The credibility of the gospel and the church will be tarnished.

Think of the devastation in your own home, your humiliated partner, with the bottom falling out of the world. You leave your spouse crippled, broken-hearted, devastated, mortified. The devastating effects never go away entirely. Untold suffering is inflicted upon family and friends. And what of your children – what of them? They will be impaired, damaged, thrust through with a terrible sword wielded by a parent's hand, leaving them torn to shreds, which all of life will never be able to heal. They will bear the scars of your selfish action to the grave.

Think of the guilt, the depression, the self-loathing that will inevitably follow. Think of the possible ostracism from those who know the Bible and its standards. You will have let Christ down, let the church down, let your family down, let your parents down, let yourself down. You become despicable in your own eyes. Think on the consequences before breaking up your own family. Is it worth it all? Ponder these things well and ask God to help you to turn away from such a foolish and devastating pathway.

How to Escape – Spirituality

Restore Spiritual Intimacy

Two cyclists journeyed from one town to another and were asked at their destination whether they had seen a particularly large and impressive building *en route*. No, they hadn't. 'But you couldn't miss it!' They had. The reason? They were lovers. They had eyes for nothing but each other and the road's essentials. So we are to meet temptation with an occupied heart. However impressive the distractions on the journey of life, we are to be engrossed in fellowship with our heavenly Lover. There must be no openings where side issues can penetrate. There must be no trailing affections, no looking over the shoulder with longing glances, no deviation from Him who has captured our hearts. Life must be filled with Christ. He must dominate the horizon. Is

He not the Lily of the Valley, the Bright and Morning Star, the Fairest of Ten Thousand? Did He not ravish your heart? He is the sweet Bridegroom of heaven whose beauty pales all else into insignificance and whose revelation to the heart eclipses all the attractions of the flesh and the pleasures of sin – is He not worthy to be loved and obeyed?

How is it possible that you are sliding into this subtle, sensuous trap? How is it possible that you are being drawn into forbidden territory, that your heart is straying from your God-given spouse? Shall I tell you? You have lost sight of Jesus!

Those times of intimate fellowship with Him where He filled your soul with glory, have somehow faded away. Your quiet times are the first to lose their vitality and meaning. You may still be reading your Bible and praying, but the intimacy of communion, the humbling, breaking revelation of God to the heart, the tears, the passion for Him and His glory which flows from such an encounter and communion, is dying. Your intimate life with God has become stale and dry. Oh, you can still preach, sing with gusto, and pray with a flow of language to which you have been accustomed and which deceives everyone into thinking that you are spiritually on the crest of the wave. No-one would know about the fractured relationship except you and God. But there, where no-one sees, is spiritual drought. When last was your heart melted at the sight of the Saviour? When last did you weep in His presence? When last were you captivated by His love? When last did you pledge your allegiance to Him, passionately, totally, irrevocably?

The thing above all else that keeps us from straying is an intensely intimate encounter and relationship with Jesus Christ. To Him you are totally committed and finally accountable. Former experiences with God will not do. The relationship must be intimate, passionate, immediate.

Eternal Light, Eternal Light,
How pure the soul must be
When placed within Thy searching sight
It shrinks not but with calm delight
Can live and look on Thee.

(Thomas Binney)

Standing in His holy presence, consumed by His all-pervading love, utterly yielded to His perfect will, wholly willing to obey His slightest suggestion, here revulsion to anything other than His purity is born, here safety from unholy intrusion is secured, here passion for His holiness and glory is kindled, here direction and purpose in life is imparted, here aspirations and longings for Christlikeness are quickened, here stability and contentment in the home is founded.

Resisting Temptation

This intimate encounter works its way through into all of life. If we are true to Jesus, we will be true to each other. We will know that when temptation knocks, it is not only the immediate family which will suffer, but we will be sinning against Him if we give in. The closer we are to Him therefore, the stronger is the bond which binds us to each other, and the more secure we rest in our relationship together.

Recognize sexual attraction
Perhaps it is only at the very beginning stages where the possibilities of anything going wrong seem fanciful and remote. Perhaps it has got to the stage where the brakes need to be applied; perhaps it's getting out of hand. The first thing is to admit to the possibilities of disaster, and to acknowledge the condition. Rationalization must end. Without the recognition, 'I must be careful'; or 'I have a problem'; or 'I am doing wrong', no remedy can be applied, for no malady is acknowledged.

Repent with sincere determination
Perhaps the heart of the gospel message can be found in Acts 20:21: 'Repentance toward God and faith toward our Lord Jesus Christ.' Repentance is paramount. Repentance is not merely being sorry for our sin, but being sorry enough to quit. Do you

really want to? Repentance is a turning around, a change of course, a reversal of conduct. An acknowledgement must be made, and a decision must be taken. Action is needed to end the relationship, and this must be followed through. Different behaviour patterns may need to be adopted. Place limits upon your freedom and redirect your normal living patterns.

Forsake in sheer obedience
'He who covers his sins shall not prosper, but whoever confesses and forsakes them will have mercy' (Prov. 28:13). 'Let the wicked forsake his way...let him return to the LORD, and He will have mercy upon him' (Isa. 55: 7). Action is not based on feelings but on obedience. You may not want to make the break. It may be painful to do so, it may be misunderstood, but if it is right to do so it must be done. You must obey God determinedly, ruthlessly – cold turkey! You are accountable to God not to the other person. Don't phone, and put the receiver down when the other person phones. Be radical; be drastic. Don't start strongly and falter quickly. Accept the pain as part of the price of disobedience. You are not conforming to some man-made rule, you are obeying God-given directives and principles. Rules won't hold you but God will. To Him you are accountable.

Resist the devil

Satan and his angels prowl the planet hunting for prey. They seek our demise and patiently work on us, waiting for the best moments to strike. Satan 'deceived Eve by his craftiness' (2 Cor. 11:3). He 'transforms himself into an angel of light' (2 Cor. 11:14). He 'deceives the whole world' (Rev. 12:9).

The first thing is to recognize the temptation as an attack of the devil. When we realize that we are locked in combat with Satan, we can take the battle position and 'resist the devil' (Jas. 4:7). God tells us to do it. We do this most effectively by using the Word of God. When Paul speaks about standing 'against the wiles of the devil' he tells us to put on the whole armour of God (Eph. 6). The one offensive weapon in that armour is the sword. We have to 'take ... the sword of the Spirit.' To 'take' it is to read it, ponder it, meditate upon it, learn it, memorize it, apply it. It then becomes a weapon in our hand.

When Jesus was tempted by Satan in the wilderness (Matt. 4:1-11), he did not call for angels to protect Him, but quoted Scripture three times. He said, 'It is written....' That was the strength of His defence. If Jesus had to resort to the Word of God to ward off and conquer Satan, how much more we!

The Psalmist knew this secret for he said, 'Your Word I have hidden in my heart, that I might not sin against You' (Ps. 119:11). The Word was his defence against sin. James says, 'Resist the devil and he will flee from you.' That is a promise made by Almighty God to you and to me. The devil can do nothing else but flee. When Jesus met him with the Word he fled. We have Christ's life within us, and when we use the very method He employed, the Spirit of God tells us distinctly that Satan has no choice but to retreat in disarray.

How do we use the Word as a sword? We take a specific promise such as, 'Therefore if the Son makes you free, ye shall be free indeed' (John 8:36), or 'sin shall not have dominion over you' (Rom. 6:14), or 'thanks be to God, who gives us the victory through our Lord Jesus Christ' (1 Cor. 15:57), and declare it to be true before all heaven and hell.

As the temptation assails you, and as the battle rages, tell God that you are trusting in His Word, that it is true, and that He cannot fail you after making such marvellous promises to you. 'Lord, you have promised to set me free – do it now as I trust you.' Repeat the Scripture promise over and over. Don't let go. Let the Word sink into your heart and stay there. Claim the truth and the power of God's Word. Declare it to be true before all the forces of evil. Tell Satan that he is a defeated foe. Tell him that you resist his insidious advances and that in the mighty name of Jesus He must flee. He is conquered. He has no claim on you, for you are the Lord's. You are His by right of creation, by purchase of blood, by glad submission of will. You are serving Him and He protects you. It is with Him that Satan has to do, and He is Satan's conqueror.

'The name of the LORD is a strong tower: the righteous run to it and are safe' (Prov. 18:10). His name is Jesus and that means Saviour. He saves from sin and Satan's power. Use this all-prevailing Name in the conflict. Jesus saves me now in the fiercest temptation.

His name is Deliverer (Rom. 11:26), and He delivers now. He delivers from the sin of wrong relationships and from the sin of an 'affair'.

He is the true Light (John 1:9) shining into my darkest struggles. 'I am the Light of the world,' He said. Shine then Jesus and banish the darkness of tension, turmoil and trauma.

He is my Redeemer (Col. 1:14), having paid the price to set me free from the entanglements of sin. Claim the power of that mighty victory at Calvary where Christ's blood was shed, and where the price for our salvation was paid. 'And they overcame him (Satan) by the blood of the Lamb' (Rev. 12:11). Plead the blood of Christ as the liberating power of God, for it was at Calvary, that Satan was defeated.

He is my Life (John 14:6) and in Him I live above the threat of failure and death. We are saved not only by His death but by His life, the life which rose triumphant from the grave. That life indwells us, empowers us, frees us. Jesus lives and He lives in us. He is the Lord of all (Acts 10:36), the Mighty God (Isa. 9:6). He is Conqueror over sin, and hell and Satan. He is 'King of kings and Lord of lords' (1 Tim. 6:15). No power can stand before Him; no, not even the power of an illicit relationship. It must give way to the consuming, cleansing power of God through the blood of Jesus. He is Emmanuel, which means 'God with us' (Matt. 1:23). What a marvellous truth – God is with us. This glorious conqueror is with us, in us, around us, and we are in Him. In Him we live and move and have our being. Looking to Him, trusting in Him, claiming His promises, resting in His victory, how can we fail to find rest and deliverance!

The Name of the Lord – what a strong tower! Here we are safe. Claim His Name, and all that it means, as your dwelling, your shelter, your safe haven. In Him we can live in safety. God says that if we abide in Him we do not constantly commit sin (1 John 3:6). We are safe in this mighty Saviour. Trust Him now to keep you. 'And this is the victory that has overcome the world – our faith' (1 John 5:4). This is not imagination, it is faith. As we keep on believing, so He keeps on delivering. He is our precious, present, powerful Saviour. He saves me now! Truly, if the Son makes you free, you will certainly be free indeed (John 8:36).

Renew mental images

'But be transformed by the renewing of your mind...' (Rom. 12: 2). From every angle the mind is under attack, for there is a battle for the mind today. We live much of our lives in our minds. 'For as he thinks in his heart, so is he' (Prov. 23:7). You are not what you think you are, but what you think – you are!

Negatively, we must not feed our minds with vivid memories and fantastic daydreams of the unavailable person. They but inflame desire, weaken resolve, dim the objective and could well reverse the decision. '...bringing every thought into captivity to the obedience of Christ' (2 Cor. 10: 5).

Positively we must renew our minds with material that will transform us. Forbidden thoughts can be expelled by consciously thrusting pure thoughts into our minds. From our thoughts spring actions, so our thoughts must lead us to purity of heart and life. Paul said: 'whatever things are true... noble... just... pure... lovely... of good report... meditate on these things' (Phil. 4: 8). That is a command which we are to obey. Refuse to allow your thoughts to dwell on forbidden ground. He urges: 'Let this mind be in you which was also in Christ Jesus' (Phil. 2:5). The psalmist cries, 'Let...the meditation of my heart be acceptable in Your sight, O Lᴏʀᴅ...' (Ps. 19:14). Godly living flows from godly thinking, and godly thinking comes from a vital, intimate relationship with Jesus Christ. It all hinges on that living contact!

Trust for delivering mercies
Faith is born in repentance: 'Ye repented not afterward that ye might believe' (Matt. 21:32, ᴀᴠ). If the repentance is real, faith can take root. Faith for what?

Surely if the relationship is seen to be wrong, it must be dissolved, and, because this is a painful and complicated issue, you need the help of the Lord to disentangle you from its entwining stranglehold. Disobedience has brought pain and discomfort, guilt and dismay, hurt and grief. That's the price. Not only is there sorrow for the hurt caused to the other party, but you have sinned against God. David said, 'Against You, You only, have I sinned' (Ps. 51:4). That's where the sorrow lies.

Firstly therefore, it is faith for *forgiveness and cleansing*. To enjoy the smile of the Lord again we need to know the blessedness of forgiveness and the joy of restoration. We need to know that we are clean. Inappropriate thoughts must be crucified.

Fantasies about the unavailable person must be completely removed. They are neither fitting, proper nor right. In fact they are sin. We have a place of cleansing, of purity, of repair, of victory. It is Calvary. Here sin is dealt with. There is power in the precious blood of Christ to remove the last vestige of sin and condemnation: '...the blood of Jesus Christ His Son cleanses us from all sin' (1 John 1:7). The verb is in the present tense. The blood keeps on cleansing, so we can be kept clean. 'If we confess our sins, He is faithful and just to forgive us our sins and to cleanse us from all unrighteousness' (1 John 1:9). As we trust, our sins are forgiven, our hearts are cleansed, our consciences are relieved, our lives are realigned. Peace returns at last. 'My peace I give to you,' said Jesus (John 14:27).

'Come now, and let us reason together,' says the LORD; 'though your sins are like scarlet, they shall be as white as snow' (Isa. 1:18).

> There is a fountain filled with blood
> Drawn from Emmanuel's veins,
> And sinners plunged beneath that flood
> Lose all their guilty stains.
>
> (William Cowper)

This leads to faith for *deliverance*. You need to know deliverance from the entanglements and intrigues of the power which has subtly held you in its sensuous grip, deliverance from sexually manipulative behaviour, from inappropriate remarks and suggestive dress and mannerisms. You need deliverance. 'Surely He shall deliver you from the snare of the fowler...' (Ps. 91:3). 'For this purpose the Son of God was manifested, that He might destroy the works of the devil' (1 John 3:8). '...with God all things are possible' (Matt. 19:26). Let's trust Him for full deliverance!

> He breaks the power of cancelled sin,
> And sets the prisoner free;
> His blood can make the foulest clean,
> His blood avails for me.
>
> (Charles Wesley)

Now, of course, we need faith for *continuance*. 'No temptation has overtaken you except such as is common to man; but God is faithful, who will not allow you to be tempted beyond what you are able, but with the temptation will also make the way of escape, that you may be able to bear it' (1 Cor. 10:13). 'And the Lord will deliver me from every evil work and preserve me for His heavenly kingdom' (2 Tim. 4:18). 'Now to Him who is able to keep you from stumbling, and to present you faultless before the presence of His glory with exceeding joy...' (Jude 24). 'He is able to keep what I have committed to Him until that day' (2 Tim. 1:12).

Able to keep! Let us take Him at His Word. He says that He will make a way to escape, that He is able to deliver, that He is able to preserve us, that He is able to keep us. He has promised these things. Can we believe that He will keep His promises if we dare to trust Him?

Let us trust His integrity and lay hold of His ability to keep His promises to us. Let's trust Him now.

Related Scriptures

Judah ... through her casual harlotry ... defiled the land.

Jeremiah 3:9

For from within, out of the heart of men, proceed evil thoughts, adulteries, fornications.... All these evil things come from within and defile a man.

Mark 7:21, 23

Let us walk properly, as in the day, not in revelry and drunkenness, not in licentiousness and lewdness.... But put on the Lord Jesus Christ, and make no provision for the flesh, to fulfil its lusts.

Romans 13:13, 14

But now I have written to you not to keep company with anyone named a brother, who is a fornicator

1 Corinthians 5:11

Do not be deceived. Neither fornicators, nor idolaters, nor adulterers, nor homosexuals, nor sodomites ... will inherit the kingdom of God

1 Corinthians 6:9, 10

Now the body is not for sexual immorality but for the Lord, and the Lord for the body

1 Corinthians 6:13

Flee sexual immorality. Every sin that a man does is outside the body, but he who commits sexual immorality sins against his own body. Or do you not know that your body is the temple of the Holy Spirit who is in you, whom you have from God, and you are not your own? For you were bought at a price; therefore glorify God in your body and in your spirit, which are God's.

1 Corinthians 6:18-20

Nor let us commit sexual immorality, as some of them did, and in one day twenty-three thousand fell.

1 Corinthians 10:8

Now the works of the flesh are evident which are: adultery, fornication, uncleanness, licentiousness ... of which I tell you beforehand, just as I also told you in time past, that those who practise such things will not inherit the kingdom of God. But the fruit of the Spirit is ... self-control.

Galatians 5:19-23

But fornication and all uncleanness ... let it not even be named among you, as is fitting for saints; neither filthiness, nor foolish talking, which are not fitting.... For this you know, that no fornicator, unclean person ... has any inheritance in the kingdom of Christ and God.

Ephesians 5:3-5

Therefore put to death ... fornication, uncleanness, passion, evil desire.... Because of these things the wrath of God is coming

Colossians 3:5, 6

For this is the will of God, your sanctification: that you should abstain from sexual immorality

1 Thessalonians 4:3

Follow peace with all men, and holiness ... lest there be any fornicator.

Hebrews 12:14, 16

Fornicators and adulterers God will judge
Hebrews 13:4

Blessed are those who do His commandments, that they may have the right to the tree of life, and may enter through the gates into the city. But outside are dogs and sorcerers and sexually immoral.
Revelation 22:14, 15

Other Books of Interest
from
Christian Focus

Sounds from Heaven

Colin & Mary Peckham

The Revival on the Isle of Lewis, 1949-1952

SY360

Sounds from Heaven

The Revival on the Isle of Lewis, 1949–1952

Colin & Mary Peckham

'…provides ringing affirmation that God is still on His throne and delights to make bare His mighty arm in revival when His people get serious with Him.'
Richard Owen Roberts, Author of *Scotland saw His Glory*

'Here you can read Duncan Campbell's own reports, along with eyewitness records (including that of Mary) of those amazing days, and a description of the characteristics of the revival. …the desperate state of our society and the church which bears the name of Christ should drive us to pray with the Psalmist, "Will You not revive us again, O Lord?"'
Peter Grainger
Senior Pastor, Charlotte Baptist Chapel, Edinburgh

'In a time of extreme apathy among Christian people, yet when talk about revival has become trendy, many Christians have no real concept of true God-sent revival. May this publication be used to provide a clearer understanding of revival and also create a longing that God, in His providence, may revive us again and awaken His Church which, in many places, has settled for death.'
Tom Shaw, Honorary President of The Faith Mission.

'I cannot recall any book on revival that I have read that has given me greater pleasure, held my attention more, and incited my longing for a new visitation from God more that this one.'
Brian Edwards

ISBN 1-85792-953-5

The Authority Of **The Bible**

'...an enormously valuable aid to all who wish to understand the significance of the Bible for today's world.'

Clive Calver,
President - World Relief
Corporation, USA

Colin Peckham

The Authority of the Bible

Colin Peckham

The Christian faith is based upon the trustworthiness of the Bible. Once the authority of Scripture is doubted then everything is just opinion. That is why the authority of the Bible is a battleground.

Yet, the reliability of Scripture is probably one of the Bible's strongest claims. Compared to all other historical manuscripts none has a better pedigree of texts in agreement, none has such extensive external evidence from writings and archaeology confirming its basic narrative. In fact no other religious document is so firmly grounded in time and place – the amazing claim of this book is that you can trust the Bible.

Dr. Colin Peckham, principal of the Faith Mission Bible College, shows the relevance of the Bible in today's multi-cultural context and how it compares with sources for Hinduism, Islam and other world religions. He also shows us Christ's attitude towards the Old Testament and how archaeology and other external evidence now establishes the trustworthiness of Biblical texts.

This is an important book to read, it clears away the misinformation of the past and re-establishes the correctness of the Bible. If you want to find out why so many people trust it then this is a great place to start.

'...an enormously valuable aid to all who wish to understand the significance of the Bible for today's world.'

Clive Calver

'In a day when the Bible is rejected or undermined ...it is gratifying to find a teacher who has no such doubts.'

**A.T.B. McGowan,
Highland Theological College, Dingwall,Scotland**

1-85792-436-3

"If you aren't careful,
religion can make you 'weird'.
This book is the antidote."
Steve Brown, Key Life Network

DOCWALK

Putting into practice what you SAY you believe

LARRY DIXON

Author of DocTALK

DocWALK

Putting into practice what you SAY you believe

Larry Dixon

C.S. Lewis said *'When we Christians behave badly, or fail to behave well, we are making Christianity unbelievable to the outside world.'*

Surveys of churchgoers reveal a huge problem – there is too little difference between them and people who don't go the church! If our beliefs are to be taken seriously then they must be seen to have a difference in our behavior.

Larry's previous book DocTALK focussed on our beliefs as Christians: DocWALK zones in on our behavior - how we put into practice what we say we believe.

Laced with practical illustrations and subversive humor, Dixon's remarkable insight highlights how doctrine makes a difference in the way we live.

'Larry Dixon has given us an "Owners Manual" for Christians. If you aren't careful, religion can make you "weird." This book is the antidote. With incredible balance and insight, Biblical faithfulness and Christian reality (mixed with delightful humor), Dr. Dixon cuts through the nonsense and the silliness and points to what it means to live an authentic Christian life. Read it. You'll be glad you did!'

Steve Brown, RTS Orlando, Key Life Network

ISBN 1-84550-052-0

Practicing Proverbs

Wise Living for Foolish Times

Richard Mayhue

This is a unique book on a unique part of Scripture. Mayhue introduces us to Solomon, the writer of Proverbs, and then gets to grips with the book itself and its message. He answers some of the most frequently asked questions about Proverbs and how the book has pressing relevance to Christians today.

Then, he re-organises the text of the entire book of Proverbs into six life applications – **spiritual, personal, family, intellectual, market-place** and **societal** each also having particular themes highlighted within them.

Practicing Proverbs is one book with multiple uses; devotional, small group discipleship book, resource for the biblical counselor and for teaching Christian ethics and morality.

'Dr. Mayhue's book fills a long-awaited need. It makes the Proverbs accessible. This is a marvelous tool for the Bible student, as well as a rich resource for every reader.'
John MacArthur

Practicing Proverbs *is one of the most practical books you will ever read! Why? Because Richard Mayhue bases his thoughts and unique arrangement of materials on one of the most helpful books of the Bible. Ever since Mayhue's conversion he has incorporated these same principles into his daily life, and with tremendous effect. You too can experience the same great blessing in your life. I would strongly encourage everyone to read this book!*
Tim LaHaye

Richard Mayhue is Executive Vice President of The Master's College and Seminary in the Los Angeles, California area.

ISBN 1-85792-777-X

A BETTER WAY

SIMON AUSTEN

JESUS AND OLD TESTAMENT FULFILMENT

A Better Way

Jesus and Old Testament fulfilment

Simon Austen

To many young people today the Bible is a closed book. Our knowledge of the Old Testament is particularly thin whilst that of the New revolves around the great Christian festivals of Christmas and Easter (with a few parables thrown in for good measure!).

When Jesus walked to Emmaus with two disciples after the resurrection he went through the Old Testament with them and showed them how it was all about him. Simon Austen has captured that joyous curiosity and amazement as he explains how the major events of the Old Testament pointed to a new era, a better way.

If you want to discover *a better way* then Simon can help you come alive to the wonder of how the purpose of history points to a person in history.

'...shows the progressive unfolding of the Bible's plot line. In a sense, each chapter is a gospel presentation, with a different starting-point in the Old Testament'.

David Peterson

'...an attractive survey of the Christ-centred truths running right through the Scriptures'

Richard Bewes

'This is a superb, engagingly written and immensely timely book'.

Dominic Smart

Simon Austen is Vicar of Houghton and Kingmoor in Carlisle, England.

ISBN 1-85792-867-9

Christian Focus Publications

publishes books for all ages

Our mission statement –

STAYING FAITHFUL

In dependence upon God we seek to help make His infallible Word, the Bible, relevant. Our aim is to ensure that the Lord Jesus Christ is presented as the only hope to obtain forgiveness of sin, live a useful life and look forward to heaven with Him.

REACHING OUT

Christ's last command requires us to reach out to our world with His gospel. We seek to help fulfill that by publishing books that point people towards Jesus and help them develop a Christ-like maturity. We aim to equip all levels of readers for life, work, ministry and mission.

Books in our adult range are published in three imprints.

Christian Focus contains popular works including biographies, commentaries, basic doctrine and Christian living. Our children's books are also published in this imprint.

Mentor focuses on books written at a level suitable for Bible College and seminary students, pastors, and other serious readers. The imprint includes commentaries, doctrinal studies, examination of current issues and church history.

Christian Heritage contains classic writings from the past.

Christian Focus Publications, Ltd
Geanies House, Fearn,
Ross-shire, IV20 1TW, Scotland, United Kingdom
info@christianfocus.com
www.christianfocus.com